SUMMARY OF PROPHESY YOUR YEAR

The Adventure of Discovering God's Voice throughout the Year

LINDSEY REIMER

D DESTINY IMAGE

Destiny Image P.O. Box 310, Shippensburg, PA 17257-0310

This book and all other Destiny Image's books are available at Christian bookstores and distributors worldwide.

For Worldwide Distribution, Printed in the U.S.A.

Reach us on the Internet: www.destinyimage.com.

ISBN 13 TP: 979-8-8815-0396-3

ISBN 13 eBook: 979-8-8815-0397-0

CONTENTS

INTRODUCTION

❦

"Prophesy Your Year" is a transformative guide that invites readers on a year-long journey of spiritual discovery and personal growth through prophetic practice. This book uniquely combines the deeply spiritual with the highly practical, guiding individuals through monthly prompts that encourage them to engage actively with God's voice in their lives. Each chapter of the summary distills insights and actionable steps from the original book, making the profound lessons accessible and applicable for everyday life.

The core premise of "Prophesy Your Year" is that each individual has the potential to connect directly with divine guidance, revealing a path that is both empowering and illuminating. Through a series of reflective questions and prompts, readers are encouraged to explore their relationship with God, uncovering the specific ways He speaks to them and the unique journey He has designed for each one.

This summary aims to encapsulate the essence of the book's teachings, presenting key themes such as identity, wonder, gratitude, and the pursuit of God's mysteries. It serves as a compass for those looking to deepen their spiritual walk and to embrace the unpredictability of life with faith and expectancy. Whether you are new to the concept of prophetic journaling or seeking to rekindle your spiritual insights, this summary offers a month-by-month guide to harnessing the power of prophecy in your personal growth and spiritual maturity.

CHAPTER 1

JANUARY

Bible Verse

"Call to me and I will answer you, and will tell you
great and hidden things that you have not known."
- Jeremiah 33:3 (ESV)

Introduction

This chapter encourages readers to actively seek God's guidance at the beginning of the year, emphasizing the importance of listening for a prophetic word that could direct their actions and attitudes throughout the year. It illustrates this through a personal testimony, providing a tangible example of how such guidance can have significant, real-world implications.

Word of Wisdom

"Sometimes we need to ask the Lord if
He is speaking metaphorically or literally.

Because, sometimes, it's literally." Lindsey Reiman

Main Theme

The main theme of this chapter is the impactful nature of seeking and receiving prophetic words from God, and how such words can manifest in both expected and unexpected ways, shaping personal circumstances significantly.

Key Points

Begin the year by asking God for guidance and a prophetic word to shape the upcoming months. Document any messages or guidance received as if it were a personal letter from God.
Recognize that prophetic words can be literal or metaphorical and may require discernment.
Prophetic acts, symbolic gestures that mirror divine instructions, can bring spiritual revelations into the physical realm.
The biblical precedent shows that prophets like Elisha and Ezekiel performed prophetic acts to convey God's message visually and symbolically.
Engage in prophetic acts with a spirit of joy and childlike curiosity to fully embrace their spiritual significance.

Key Themes

- **Seeking Divine Guidance:** At the start of the year, it is beneficial to seek specific direction from God, which can help align one's personal goals and actions with divine will, as demonstrated by Russell's profound testimony of being forewarned about his health challenges.
- **Literal and Metaphorical Interpretations:** Prophetic messages often require interpretation; they can be straightforward or symbolic, and understanding their nature is crucial for appropriate response and preparation, as seen in the unexpected literal fulfillment of a prophetic warning.
- **Recording and Reflecting on Prophetic Words:** Writing down what is perceived as a message from God acts as a tangible reference and can provide comfort and guidance, especially during challenging times, highlighting the power of recorded words.
- **The Role of Prophetic Acts:** These acts are more than rituals; they are a form of obedience that can lead to spiritual breakthroughs, mirroring the biblical examples where physical actions led to spiritual and societal changes.
- **Childlike Engagement with the Prophetic:** Approaching prophetic acts with innocence and openness can transform these experiences from mechanical exercises to meaningful

spiritual engagements that resonate deeply and produce significant impacts.

- **Historical and Scriptural Foundations:** The biblical narratives provide a rich history of prophets using dramatic, visual methods to deliver God's messages, reinforcing the validity and power of engaging in prophetic acts in contemporary faith practices.

Conclusion

Engaging with God through asking for and acting on prophetic words is a profound practice that bridges the spiritual and physical realms. This chapter not only guides individuals on how to approach prophetic acts but also reassures them of the legitimacy and potential life-changing impact of these divine interactions. By incorporating these practices, believers can experience a more dynamic and guided spiritual life.

CHAPTER 2

FEBRUARY

Bible Verse

"Therefore encourage one another and build each other up, just as in fact you are doing." – 1 Thessalonians 5:11 (NIV)

Introduction

This chapter invites readers to explore the relational aspect of God's nature, particularly during February, a month often associated with relationships. Rather than focusing solely on romantic relationships, the emphasis here is on all kinds—family, friends, coworkers, and future connections. Readers are encouraged to seek God's guidance on how to bless and strengthen these relationships through prayer and a prophetic act. The chapter also introduces the concept of prophesying signs as a way of receiving and recognizing God's messages, grounding this practice in biblical examples.

Word of Wisdom

"God is moving throughout my day more than I realize. He is moving, and we aren't catching it because we are human and we have finite brains." Lindsey Reiman

Main Theme

The main theme of this chapter centers on strengthening relationships by seeking God's guidance and performing prophetic acts, while also learning to recognize and prophesy signs as confirmations of God's word in one's life.

Key Points

- God calls us to relationships that will further His purpose and bring unity.
- Prayer can be a powerful tool to bless relationships and deepen bonds.
- Prophetic acts serve as tangible expressions of our prayers for others.
- Signs are God's language and are meant to point us toward Jesus and His will.
- Prophesying signs requires practice and builds our faith and awareness of God's involvement in our lives.
- Biblical examples of signs show how they serve as confirmations of God's promises.

Key Themes

- **God-Centered Relationships**: Relationships are central to God's design and purpose for us. When we seek His direction, we find ways to bless and strengthen these connections, allowing them to reflect God's love and unity.
- **Power of Prophetic Acts**: Performing a prophetic act, such as praying over a loved one's belongings, can serve as a symbolic extension of our faith, asking God's presence to bring peace, healing, or encouragement.
- **Biblical Basis for Signs**: The Bible provides examples of signs that confirm God's word, like the shadow moving back for Hezekiah, demonstrating that signs are an integral part of His communication with us.
- **Learning to Recognize Signs**: As we practice prophesying signs, we develop an awareness of how God speaks in our daily lives. This practice builds our spiritual sensitivity and deepens our relationship with God.
- **God's Desire for Our Flourishing**: God's signs are not only guidance but are reminders of His desire for our well-being. Recognizing signs can reinforce that God values our wholeness and peace, even in the small, unexpected moments.

Conclusion

This chapter encourages readers to view February as a time to deepen and bless relationships through prayer and intentional actions. By inviting God's presence into our relationships and practicing the prophesying of signs, we can gain greater insight into His active role in our lives. As we cultivate the skill of listening for God's signs, we also build a foundation of faith, trusting that He continually works for our good and calls us into relationships that reflect His divine love and purpose.

CHAPTER 3

MARCH

Bible Verse

"For we know in part and we prophesy in part." 1 Corinthians 13:9 (NIV)

Introduction

March invites readers to introspectively consider what they are moving towards spiritually, emotionally, or physically, and to seek divine guidance for their journey. This chapter emphasizes understanding God's plans through prophetic words and signs, and integrating insights from personal reflection and community input.

Word of Wisdom

"God doesn't hide things from us, He hides things for us." Lindsey Reiman

Main Theme

The main theme is exploring and understanding the forward movement in one's life through the lens of spiritual, emotional, or physical progression with the help of prophetic guidance.

Key Points

- Inquire of the Lord about areas of personal advancement for the month, whether spiritual, emotional, or physical.
- Identify prophetic words that resonate with your current life direction.
- Look for signs that confirm and illuminate these prophetic words.
- Recognize the collective aspect of prophecy, where community and shared insights play crucial roles.
- Approach prophecies with curiosity and openness, looking for connections and confirmations.
- Value the input from others as potentially fitting pieces of your personal prophetic puzzle.

Key Themes

- **Interpreting Prophetic Guidance:** This chapter guides readers to ask for and interpret prophetic words concerning their current or future paths, encouraging them to see these words as divine guidance for their personal journey. Signs are given special emphasis as confirmations of these words, acting as markers that one is on the right path.

- **Community's Role in Prophecy:** Prophetic insights often come not just through individual prayer but through community interaction, where others contribute pieces of a larger divine puzzle. This process underlines the importance of the body of Christ in helping each individual discern their trajectory.
- **The Puzzle of Prophecy:** Prophecy is described as assembling a puzzle, where each piece, whether from personal prayer or another's word, contributes to a fuller understanding of God's will. This metaphor encourages readers to consider how different pieces of prophecy fit together to form a clearer picture.
- **Curiosity and Discernment in Prophecy:** The chapter encourages a balance of curiosity about prophetic words and prudent discernment in interpreting them. It emphasizes that while not every prophetic word will directly apply or need immediate action, all should be considered thoughtfully and prayerfully.
- **Integration of Prophetic Signs:** The integration of prophetic signs into one's spiritual practice is detailed, suggesting that signs not only guide but also encourage believers as they witness God's active presence in their lives. This reassurance is crucial for spiritual confidence and growth.

Conclusion

March challenges readers to consciously consider what they are advancing towards in their lives and to actively seek God's guidance through prophetic words and signs. By weaving together personal insights with those from their spiritual community, individuals can gain a more comprehensive understanding of their path forward. This chapter empowers readers to embrace their journey with divine foresight and community support, turning prophetic insights into actionable steps in their personal and communal lives.

CHAPTER 4

APRIL

Bible Verse

"Every matter must be established by the testimony of two or three witnesses." - 2 Corinthians 13:1 (NIV)

Introduction

April's theme is about nurturing and cultivating areas of life that require attention, encouraging readers to inquire of the Holy Spirit, "What needs watering this month?" This process involves identifying aspects of life that need nurture—be it personal, financial, or spiritual.

Word of Wisdom

"Believe me, I decided to pay close attention to my spending and taxes that month!" Lindsey Reiman

. . .

Main Theme

The main theme is focused on identifying and nurturing areas in one's life that need attention and cultivation, using prophetic guidance to recognize and act on these needs.

Key Points

- Inquire about what areas of your life need nurturing or attention this month.
- Understand that "watering" can mean providing care, effort, or focus to different aspects of life.
- Use prophetic guidance to identify specific actions or attentions required.
- Look for signs as confirmations of what has been revealed through prophetic words.
- Recognize and interpret patterns in prophetic words and signs as guidance.
- Maintain faith and persistence in seeking and recognizing divine signs, even when they are delayed.

Key Themes

- **Prophetic Inquiry and Personal Growth:** By asking what needs watering, individuals are encouraged to reflect on areas in their life that require growth or attention. This could be emotional, such as relationships, or practical, such as financial diligence, with prophetic insight guiding the process.

- **Signs as Confirmations of Action:** Signs are not just supernatural occurrences but are often everyday happenings that, when observed closely, act as confirmations of the divine guidance received. This chapter teaches the importance of staying alert and recognizing these signs in everyday life.
- **Integration of Community Insights:** The prophetic process is often communal, involving insights from others that can provide additional guidance or confirmation. This reinforces the importance of community in spiritual growth and discernment.
- **Patterns as Divine Clues:** Recognizing patterns in prophetic words and signs helps to piece together a clearer picture of God's direction. This methodical approach to prophecy encourages believers to track and piece together various prophetic inputs over time.
- **Persistence in Faith and Recognition:** The teaching emphasizes persistence in recognizing and responding to prophetic signs, encouraging believers to remain engaged and attentive to divine communication, regardless of timing or immediate clarity.

Conclusion

April calls for a focused effort on parts of one's life that need nurturing, guided by prophetic insights and confirmed through signs. This chapter encourages a proactive stance in spiritual listening and observation, urging readers to identify, nurture, and cultivate the areas highlighted by the Holy Spirit. Through examples and teachings, it provides a framework for understanding how to integrate divine guidance into practical life changes, fostering both personal and communal spiritual growth.

CHAPTER 5

MAY

Bible Verse

"To all who mourn in Israel, he will give a crown of beauty for ashes, a joyous blessing instead of mourning, festive praise instead of despair." - Isaiah 61:3 (NIV)

Introduction

This chapter invites readers to explore the concept of beauty in their lives, prompting them to ask what needs nurture or attention and how beauty can be perceived in various aspects, whether through nature, trials, or everyday experiences.

Word of Wisdom

"He produces beauty in all of it; in fact, He even gives beauty for ashes."
Lindsey Reiman

Main Theme

The theme centers on the pursuit of recognizing and appreciating the beauty that God creates around and within us, regardless of its form—external, internal, or abstract.

Key Points

- Ask the Holy Spirit what in your life needs nurturing or "watering" this month.
- Consider how beauty can manifest in various forms and experiences.
- Reflect on the role of beauty in enhancing spiritual understanding and appreciation.
- Seek signs from God as confirmations of where to focus your efforts on finding beauty.
- Recognize the transformative power of beauty, especially in challenging circumstances.
- Engage in spiritual reflection to better understand the significance of beauty in your personal growth.

Key Themes

- **Beauty in Transformation:** The chapter discusses how beauty is not only external but also emerges from within challenging experiences, transforming trials into testimonies. This transformation is akin to the biblical promise of receiving beauty for ashes, which underscores God's redemptive power in our lives.

- **Prophetic Guidance on Beauty:** Through personal stories and biblical examples, the text illustrates how prophetic insights can lead to a deeper appreciation of beauty in unlikely places. Readers are encouraged to seek and recognize these prophetic messages as guides to uncovering beauty.
- **The Role of Nature in Understanding God:** The narrative suggests that nature itself is a canvas of God's artistic expression, offering insights into His character as the Creator. This perspective helps to align one's appreciation of beauty with spiritual reverence and understanding.
- **Beauty and Spiritual Identity:** Exploring beauty can also be a journey into understanding one's spiritual identity, as seen through the transformation of biblical figures who discovered their true selves in God's narrative for their lives. This theme emphasizes the link between recognizing beauty and embracing one's identity in Christ.
- **Community and Confirmation:** The importance of community in affirming and supporting one's journey towards recognizing beauty is highlighted. Testimonies and shared experiences serve as confirmations and encouragement, reinforcing the collective aspect of spiritual growth.

Conclusion

May is a month for recognizing the diverse manifestations of beauty that God brings into our lives. This chapter guides readers to engage with this theme proactively, encouraging them to see beyond the surface and appreciate the deeper beauty in all things. Through personal inquiry, prophetic insight, and communal support, readers are led to a greater appreciation of the beauty that surrounds them and the beauty they are capable of cultivating within themselves.

CHAPTER 6

JUNE

Bible Verse

"See what great love the Father has lavished on us, that we should be called children of God! And that is what we are!" - 1 John 3:1 (NIV)

Introduction

This chapter emphasizes the profound importance of understanding and embracing one's identity in God, with a specific focus on how individuals are operating within that identity during the current month. It encourages readers to recognize how deeply they are loved and valued by God.

Word of Wisdom

"He not only loves you, He likes you!"
Lindsey Reiman

Main Theme

The main theme explores the concept of identity in God—how it is understood, embraced, and manifested in daily life, particularly focusing on how one is uniquely operating within this identity at the present time.

Key Points

- Inquire of God about your specific identity and how you are manifesting it in the current month.
- Seek divine confirmation through a sign that reaffirms this understanding of your identity.
- Reflect on God's love and delight in you as foundational aspects of your identity.
- Investigate any previous prophetic words to identify patterns or repeated themes related to your identity.
- Be vigilant for future prophetic words that may further elucidate or confirm aspects of your divine identity.
- Embrace the dynamic nature of how you might operate differently in your identity during various seasons of life.

Key Themes

- **Dynamic Nature of Divine Identity:**
  This chapter illustrates that identity in God is not static but dynamic, changing as

one grows and moves through different life phases and challenges. It underscores that at different times, a person may embody various aspects of their identity, such as being a 'Disruptor' in one season and perhaps a 'Healer' in another.

- **Prophetic Guidance on Identity:** Through personal engagement and divine conversation, individuals are guided to deeper self-awareness and understanding. The prophetic process is emphasized as a tool for discovering and confirming one's divine role and purpose, encouraging readers to seek and pay attention to how God communicates their identity to them.
- **Foundational Love and Acceptance:** Recognizing that God's love is the foundation of identity is central to this chapter. It challenges readers to see themselves as God sees them, loved and appreciated, which can transform self-perception and enhance spiritual and emotional well-being.
- **Pattern Recognition in Prophetic Words:** The text advises maintaining a record of prophetic words and actively looking for patterns that may help clarify and confirm one's identity in God. This practice is presented as a method to piece together divine messages over time, providing clearer direction and deeper understanding.
- **Operational Aspects of Identity:** Each person's identity in God includes operational elements—how they are to act, interact, and react in accordance with

divine guidance. This chapter encourages exploration of what actions are being called for in the current period and how they align with one's broader divine identity.

Conclusion

June calls for a deep dive into the personal discovery of how one is living out their identity in God at the moment. It emphasizes the love and delight that God has for each individual, encouraging them to see themselves through His eyes. By engaging with prophetic insights and seeking signs of confirmation, readers are invited to embrace a fuller understanding of their divine identity and operate within it with confidence and faith. This exploration is not only about personal growth but also about aligning more closely with God's purposes for one's life.

CHAPTER 7

JULY

Bible Verse

"This is the day the Lord has made; we will rejoice and be glad in it." - Psalm 118:24 (NKJV)

Introduction

This chapter encourages readers to embrace and celebrate the small, seemingly insignificant moments of life with the same enthusiasm as the larger victories. It inspires a mindset shift to appreciate daily blessings through a narrative about a seer prophet who found wonder in a speck of glitter.

Word of Wisdom

"Children get excited and celebrate the things before them without needing proof. They respond with pure joy to the small, simple moments." Lindsey Reiman

Main Theme

The main theme is about cultivating a spirit of celebration in all aspects of life, recognizing both minor and significant achievements or experiences as reasons to rejoice.

Key Points

• Inquire of God about what to celebrate this month, big or small.

• Embrace a childlike wonder in celebrating everyday moments.

• Recognize the presence of God's glory in simple, everyday occurrences.

• Acknowledge every small success or moment of joy as a gift.

• Reflect on the significance of your existence and the inherent value of life.

• Celebrate the spiritual and relational growth no matter the scale.

Key Themes

• **Finding Joy in Simplicity:** This chapter highlights the importance of finding joy in the small, everyday details of life, encouraging a perspective that sees divine wonder in all things. It argues that true contentment and joy come from appreciating the simple blessings, not just waiting for big achievements.

- **Celebration as a Spiritual Practice:** By framing celebration as a spiritual practice, the text invites readers to integrate gratitude and joy into their daily lives. This practice helps to cultivate a positive outlook and can transform mundane experiences into moments of spiritual significance.
- **God's Presence in the Mundane:** The narrative encourages readers to recognize signs of God's presence in everyday life, much like the prophet who saw God's glory in a piece of glitter. This awareness can lead to a more fulfilled and spiritually aware life.
- **Impact of Attitude on Perception:** The chapter teaches that an attitude of celebration can change one's perception of their circumstances. Celebrating small victories and moments can lead to a greater appreciation of life's journey and the growth that comes with it.
- **The Role of Faith in Celebration:** Emphasizing faith, the text connects the ability to celebrate small moments with a deep trust in God's plan. It suggests that faith enhances the capacity to find joy in all circumstances, echoing the biblical call to rejoice always.

Conclusion

July's message is a call to celebrate life's every moment with the joy and wonder of a child. It challenges readers to shift their focus from solely monumental achievements to also embrace and rejoice in the daily gifts of life. By doing so, believers can live more fulfilling lives, grounded in gratitude and amplified by the joy of everyday blessings.

CHAPTER 8
AUGUST

Bible Verse
"To everything there is a season, a time for every purpose under heaven." - Ecclesiastes 3:1 (NKJV)

Introduction

This chapter encourages readers to embrace the natural cycles of beginnings and endings, reflecting the biblical principle that life's seasons are orchestrated by God. It challenges individuals to consider what is concluding and what is starting anew in their lives.

Word of Wisdom

"Sometimes you don't know where you are going—you just know where you can't stay." Lindsey Reiman

Main Theme

The theme of August is to identify and accept the phases of ending and beginning in various aspects of life, recognizing them as opportunities for growth and renewal orchestrated by God's divine timing.

Key Points

• Ask God to reveal what is ending and what is beginning in your life this month.

• Understand that recognizing endings and beginnings can lead to personal growth and new opportunities.

• Be open to the natural cycle of life that includes both joys and challenges.

• Acknowledge that change often requires letting go of the past to embrace the future.

• Reflect on how previous transitions have shaped your life and spiritual journey.

• Embrace the discomfort of the unknown as part of God's plan for your development.

Key Themes

• **Divine Choreography of Life's Seasons:** The chapter illustrates that life's transitions are not random but are parts of a divine choreography. Each phase, whether an ending or a beginning, plays a crucial role in God's plan for personal and spiritual development.

- **Spiritual Significance of Letting Go:** Emphasizing the need to let go of past seasons to embrace new beginnings, the text encourages readers to see the spiritual significance in endings as much as in beginnings. This perspective helps individuals to move forward with hope and acceptance rather than regret.
- **Finding God's Purpose in Transitions:** By engaging in dialogue with God about life's transitions, individuals can gain insight into His purposes for their current circumstances. This process is not just about change but about understanding the deeper reasons behind why things must start or end.
- **The Role of Faith in Uncertain Times:** The chapter highlights the role of faith when navigating endings and new beginnings. Faith is portrayed as a guiding light that helps believers to trust in God's timing and plan, even when the path ahead is unclear.
- **Celebration as a Response to Life's Rhythms:** Drawing from the idea of celebrating both small and significant moments, the narrative encourages a stance of joy and gratitude for all experiences. Celebrating transitions as part of God's glorious design leads to a more fulfilling and spiritually enriched life.

Conclusion

August is a call to actively engage with the cycles of life, recognizing and honoring both the endings and the beginnings as essential parts of God's plan. Through prayerful inquiry and a reflective approach, readers are encouraged to embrace the transitions, finding beauty and purpose in them. This chapter serves as a reminder of the continuous movement of life and the perpetual presence of God in guiding through each season, encouraging a celebratory attitude towards life's inevitable changes.

CHAPTER 9

SEPTEMBER

Bible Verse

"Draw near to God, and he will draw near to you." -
James 4:8 (ESV)

Introduction

In September, the focus is on setting aside intentional time for a divine appointment with God, much like one would schedule time with a close friend or loved one. This month encourages developing a personal relationship with God through a scheduled "date" to experience His presence and voice more intimately.

Word of Wisdom

*"No need to get religious or fretful...
let's keep it light and lovely as a date
should be." Lindsey Reiman*

Main Theme

The main theme is about deepening one's relationship with God by intentionally setting time apart to be with Him, listening for His guidance, and following through with the divine appointments set.

Key Points

• Set a specific date for a personal time with God and protect that time on your calendar.

• Approach this time with an expectation to hear from God about specific directions or blueprints for your life.

• Be flexible and open to rescheduling if life events interfere, maintaining a guilt-free attitude.

• Record insights and instructions received during this time to reflect on and act upon.

• Use this date as an opportunity to practice listening closely to God's voice and directions.

• Celebrate any manifestation of God's presence or voice during this time as a form of spiritual intimacy.

Key Themes

• **Intimacy with God through Scheduled Time:** This chapter promotes the idea of deepening one's spiritual life by scheduling regular, intentional times with God. It suggests that setting dates with God is as important as making time for any significant relationship, emphasizing that this practice can lead to profound spiritual insights and growth.

- **Listening for Divine Directions:** By dedicating time to be with God and listen, individuals can receive specific guidance and blueprints for their lives. This practice is not only about enjoying God's presence but also about actively seeking His will and direction for one's daily activities and decisions.
- **Flexibility and Non-Guilt in Spiritual Practices:** The text encourages a relaxed and flexible approach to spending time with God, advising that rescheduling due to unforeseen circumstances should not lead to guilt. This promotes a healthy relationship with God based on grace rather than rigid religious obligations.
- **Recording and Reflecting on Divine Insights:** Keeping a record of what God speaks during these times is crucial. It serves as a reminder of His words and helps in aligning one's actions with divine insight, thereby integrating spiritual experiences into practical life changes.
- **Celebration of Small Revelations:** Celebrating every small interaction or revelation during these times reinforces the joy and value found in the relationship with God. It teaches that every moment spent in God's presence is precious and worth cherishing.

Conclusion

September's lesson is to foster a closer relationship with God through scheduled divine rendezvous, where listening and responsiveness to God's voice are practiced. This approach not only enriches one's spiritual life but also embeds a deeper sense of purpose and direction in everyday living. By embracing and acting on divine insights received during these times, believers can navigate their spiritual journeys with more clarity and conviction.

CHAPTER 10

OCTOBER

Bible Verse

"Take my yoke upon you and learn from me, for I am gentle and humble in heart, and you will find rest for your souls." - Matthew 11:29 (NIV)

Introduction

This chapter is an invitation to engage in a focused inquiry into what God is teaching us individually. It challenges readers to ask God about the specific areas of knowledge or understanding He is guiding them towards in their current season of life.

Word of Wisdom

"Learning is an active, deliberate process, requiring us to be open and aware of the wisdom that surrounds us."
Lindsey Reiman

Main Theme

The central theme is the exploration of divine education—how God instructs us in unique ways that resonate with our personal journey and spiritual growth.

Key Points

• Inquire of God about what specific lessons or knowledge He wants you to learn this month.

• Reflect on any symbolic images or recurring thoughts that might indicate areas of spiritual or personal development.

• Commit to engaging deeply with the insights or teachings God reveals.

• Document your learning experiences and insights as a way to track your spiritual growth.

• Remain open and humble, recognizing that learning is a continuous process guided by God.

• Embrace the journey of learning as a dynamic interaction with the divine, full of unexpected discoveries and challenges.

Key Themes

• **Personalized Divine Curriculum:** This chapter emphasizes that God has a personalized learning plan for each believer, tailored to their unique spiritual needs and life circumstances. It encourages readers to seek God's guidance on what they should focus their learning efforts on, whether it be theological concepts, personal character development, or understanding divine mysteries.

- **The Role of Symbols and Images in Learning:** Often, God communicates through symbols and images that resonate with personal or cultural significance. The text encourages exploring these symbols as part of understanding God's specific lessons and directions, suggesting that such symbols can provide deep insights into one's spiritual journey.

- **Integrating Learning into Daily Life:** The idea of learning from God is not limited to intellectual pursuit but involves integrating divine truths into everyday life. The chapter discusses how this integration can transform routine experiences into profound spiritual lessons.

- **Humility as the Foundation of Learning:** Acknowledging that true learning requires humility, the narrative advises readers to maintain a teachable spirit. This openness is portrayed as essential for receiving and benefiting from God's wisdom.

- **Documenting Spiritual Insights:** Keeping a journal or record of what is learned during this time is recommended as a way to reflect on and solidify understanding. This practice is also a tool for recognizing how far one has come in their spiritual journey and how the teachings have been applied in real life.

Conclusion

October is presented as a month to delve into a focused learning experience with God, exploring the specific areas He wants to reveal and teach. By actively engaging with this divine curriculum, believers can deepen their understanding of God's Kingdom, their personal identity in Christ, and the practical outworking of these truths in their daily lives. This chapter encourages an adventurous and open approach to learning, where each lesson is seen as a step closer

CHAPTER 11

NOVEMBER

Bible Verse

"Give thanks in all circumstances; for this is the will of God in Christ Jesus for you." - 1 Thessalonians 5:18 (ESV)

Introduction

November's prompt challenges individuals to confront their fears of disappointment by focusing on thankfulness. This chapter encourages readers to ask, "What will I be thankful for by the time this month rolls around?" and to embrace even the potential for disappointment as part of their spiritual growth.

Word of Wisdom

"Cast your fears aside like old bait, trusting that with God as our Guide, we're fishing in waters where every catch is

meant to nourish and strengthen our faith." Lindsey Reiman

Main Theme

The main theme explores the concept of facing fears of disappointment by fostering a spirit of thankfulness and recognizing God's continual goodness, regardless of outcomes.

Key Points

• Challenge yourself to anticipate what you might be thankful for at the month's end.

• Write down everything you anticipate with hope, regardless of how unlikely it may seem.

• Reflect on your emotional response to your list—whether it's hope, fear, or gratitude.

• Revisit your list throughout the month to mark progress and shifts in perspective.

• Embrace this exercise as a spiritual practice to deepen trust in God's plan.

• Celebrate the small and big blessings as they unfold throughout the month.

Key Themes

• **Confronting Fear of Disappointment:**
  This chapter delves into the common fear of disappointment and encourages

embracing it as a pathway to deeper faith and reliance on God. It suggests that acknowledging and writing down fears can transform anxiety into anticipation and gratitude.

- **Cultivating a Thankful Heart:** The practice of predicting and reflecting on future thankfulness helps cultivate a heart that finds joy and gratitude in God's provision. This approach shifts focus from current worries to future praises, enhancing spiritual resilience.

- **Emotional Engagement with Hope and Gratitude:** By actively engaging with their emotions in response to what they hope to be thankful for, readers can gain insights into their own faith journey and emotional health. This process encourages a deeper connection with self and with God.

- **The Role of Documentation in Spiritual Growth:** Keeping a record of anticipated blessings and reflecting on them over time can provide concrete evidence of God's faithfulness. This practice not only builds faith but also serves as a testament to God's active presence in one's life.

- **Thankfulness as a Tool for Spiritual Warfare:** This theme asserts that thankfulness is not just a passive attitude but an active weapon against despair and fear. By choosing to focus on future thankfulness, believers can protect their hearts from doubt and strengthen their spiritual fortitude.

Conclusion

November's focus on what to be thankful for serves as a profound tool for spiritual growth and combating fear of disappointment. It encourages readers to trust in God's goodness and to see every situation through the lens of thankfulness. This perspective shift promises to transform fears into testimonies of faith, as believers learn to navigate life's uncertainties with a thankful heart.

CHAPTER 12

DECEMBER

Bible Verse

"Many, Lord my God, are the wonders you have done, the things you planned for us. None can compare with you; were I to speak and tell of your deeds, they would be too many to declare." - Psalm 40:5 (NIV)

Introduction

December's chapter invites readers to rediscover the gift of wonder during what is often described as the most wonderful time of the year. It emphasizes the importance of maintaining a sense of awe and curiosity in our relationship with God and the world around us.

Word of Wisdom

"Wonder motivates curiosity, cultivates gratitude, fosters imagination and innovation, and it drives us to learn more

about God and the world around us."
Lindsey Reiman

Main Theme

This chapter focuses on the essential role of wonder in the spiritual and everyday life, encouraging readers to seek and nurture this quality throughout the holiday season and beyond.

Key Points

• Reflect on what makes you experience wonder and how you can actively seek it out.

• Consider what actions or changes in perspective might enhance your sense of wonder.

• Explore the ways in which children embody and express wonder, using them as a model.

• Recognize the barriers that may be hindering your capacity for wonder, such as cynicism or busyness.

• Commit to a specific action or practice during December that will help cultivate wonder.

• Document experiences of wonder to remind yourself of its value and presence in your life.

Key Themes

• **The Nurturing of Wonder:** This chapter argues that wonder is not merely an emotional response but a spiritual discipline that enhances our perception of the divine and the mundane. It suggests practical ways to cultivate wonder, such as spending time in nature, engaging with art, or practicing mindfulness.

- **Wonder as a Defense Against Cynicism:** In a world often weighed down by skepticism and disillusionment, wonder serves as a vital counterforce that can restore joy and appreciation. The chapter discusses how maintaining a sense of wonder can lead to a more fulfilling and spiritually enriched life.
- **The Role of Environment in Fostering Wonder:** The settings in which we find ourselves can greatly influence our ability to feel wonder. The chapter encourages readers to create environments that inspire awe, whether through decor, music, or the company of inspiring individuals.
- **Learning from Children:** Children naturally exhibit wonder, and the chapter encourages adults to learn from their unabashed curiosity and enthusiasm. It discusses how adopting a childlike perspective can reopen adults' eyes to the beauty and mystery of the world.
- **The Spiritual Implications of Wonder:** Wonder connects deeply with our faith, enhancing our understanding of God's majesty and the depth of His creation. This theme explores how wonder can deepen our faith and expand our understanding of scripture and divine mysteries.

Conclusion

The chapter concludes by emphasizing that wonder is essential to a vibrant life and spiritual vitality. It challenges readers to pursue wonder actively during December and to make it a permanent fixture in their lives. By engaging with the world and God in a spirit of awe and gratitude, we can transform our everyday experiences into moments of profound insight and joy.